Balance as Belief

Johns Hopkins: Poetry and Fiction
John T. Irwin, General Editor

Poetry Titles in the Series

. . .

John Hollander, *"Blue Wine" and Other Poems*
Robert Pack, *Waking to My Name: New and Selected Poems*
Philip Dacey, *The Boy under the Bed*
Wyatt Prunty, *The Times Between*
Barry Spacks, *Spacks Street: New and Selected Poems*
Gibbons Ruark, *Keeping Company*
David St. John, *Hush*
Wyatt Prunty, *What Women Know, What Men Believe*
Adrien Stoutenberg, *Land of Superior Mirages:*
    New and Selected Poems
John Hollander, *In Time and Place*
Charles Martin, *Steal the Bacon*
John Bricuth, *The Heisenberg Variations*
Tom Disch, *Yes, Let's: New and Selected Poems*
Wyatt Prunty, *Balance as Belief*

Wyatt Prunty

Balance as Belief

The Johns Hopkins University Press
Baltimore and London

This book has been brought to publication with the generous assistance of the
G. Harry Pouder Fund and the Albert Dowling Trust.

The Johns Hopkins University Press
701 West 40th Street
Baltimore, Maryland 21211
The Johns Hopkins Press Ltd., London

The paper used in this publication meets the minimum requirements of
American National Standard for Information Sciences—Permanence of Paper
for Printer Library Materials, ANSI Z39.48-1984.

Library of Congress Cataloging in Publication Data will be found at the end
of this book.

for Eugenia, Mimi, and Holly

Contents

. . .

Acknowledgments   xi

I
Learning the Bicycle   3
The Wild Horses   4
The Shortwave Radio   6
Falling through the Ice   7
The Covined Bird   8
Water   11
The Hand-me-down   12
Driving Out   13
The Name   14
Dr. Williams' Garden   16
The Starlings   17

II
To Be Sung on the
   Fourth of July   21
Locals and Others   24
Memorial Day   26
1957   27
Good Buses   28
The Bed   29
The Actuarial Wife   30
Playing by Ear   31
The Fear   32
The Circle Route   33
Home   34
The Only Child   35
The Lean and the Fat   36

III
Crosswords 43
Late Days 44
Recalling Summers 45
For Don, Who Slept through the War 46
Doing the Numbers 47
With Others 48
The Blue Umbrella 50
Good-bye 52
The Lake House 57
Rio 62

Acknowledgments

. . .

A number of poems in this volume appeared, some in slightly
different form, in the following periodicals, to whose editors
grateful acknowledgment is made: *American Scholar:* "Learning the
Bicycle"; *Boulevard:* "The Shortwave Radio" and "The Starlings";
Kenyon Review: "The Wild Horses," "Playing by Ear," "For Don,
Who Slept through the War," "With Others," and "The Blue
Umbrella"; *Missouri Review:* "Home"; *New Criterion:* "The Bed";
Reaper: "The Covined Bird" and "The Name"; *Southern Review:*
"Falling through the Ice," "Water," "Dr. Williams' Garden,"
and "Late Days"; *Southwest Review:* "The Only Child"; and *Yale
Review:* "The Lake House."

I

Learning the Bicycle

. . .

for Heather

The older children pedal past
Stable as little gyros, spinning hard
To supper, bath, and bed, until at last
We also quit, silent and tired
Beside the darkening yard where trees
Now shadow up instead of down.
Their predictable lengths can only tease
Her as, head lowered, she walks her bike alone
Somewhere between her wanting to ride
And her certainty she will always fall.

Tomorrow, though I will run behind,
Arms out to catch her, she'll tilt then balance wide
Of my reach, till distance makes her small,
Smaller, beyond the place I stop and know
That to teach her I had to follow
And when she learned I had to let her go.

The Wild Horses

. . .

The horses imagined by a boy
Who cannot get himself to sleep
Are grazing so deep within a story
He cannot say what it means to keep
Such things inside and at a distance;
They are a silent governance
He feels but cannot name.
The horses change, and are the same.
They run miles farther than the meadows
In which he sees them run. They have no shadows,
Are unceasing, and they never die.
What he feels when watching them is like a cry
Heard somewhere else, and neither pain
Nor happiness in it, but sustained
Like a long note played in an empty room.
And that is how he waits for sleep, which soon
Takes him deeper than the fastest animal
As he tunnels clockwise in a fall,
The meadows rising through him, then gone
Somewhere above, until alone
He sees the horses turn in one long curve
That rounds them back where nothing moves,
And he knows that they were always blind,
Running from what they heard each time
The wind would shift, running away
Because they could not see their way.

To him, the horses are beautiful and sad;
They are a celebration made
Out of the way they end, begin again,
A morning's bright imperative sustained
Long after dark. They are a walling out
By looking in, what opens when he shuts
His eyes, the body's quiet allegory
By which it knows itself, a story
Told against the body that it cannot see.
The horses run because they're free
And incomplete, while poised somewhere between
The half-light in the hall and what he's seen
Inside, the boy wakes or sleeps, or turns against
His sleep, naming a larger self that rests
Invisibly, yet in sight of what it sees,
Rests without feeling, in the calculated ease
Of someone small, afraid, and fragile,
Alone and looking out, flexed but agile.

The Shortwave Radio
. . .

Unboxed on my seventh birthday
And dumb as my father's lifting arms,
It needed wires inside and out,
Plus earphones for listening late
At night, when the others were asleep.
And so we strung the copper wire
One hundred fifty feet, a giant L
Lettering our best guess overhead.
Then, ground wire set, we sat—
So many countries, their capitals
Arranged across the dial's green face,
Which warmed like an itch that only turning
Satisfied. We gazed, our headphones
Silencing like concentrated mufflers,
As we listened separately to one voice,
A pilot, like my father, lost,
The radar missing him,
                              hours lost
And you could hear it in his voice,
Although he chose his words neutrally
As he quoted altitude, fuel, landmarks,
Then course and speed.
                              But nothing worked
Except the plane, which took him farther
Every time he spoke, talking the way
We go, in casual measurements.
The goofy headphones sagged from their
Adjustments, as we leaned into the dial;
And when at last there was no answer, my father
Looked up, looked off, lit up, half smiled.

Falling through the Ice
· · ·

This, one of our oldest tales—
Late winter and the boy who skates
Ahead in darkness, staying out late
With his thin-voiced friends from school who sail
Over the ice till someone calls them home
And now, turned last, the one drops from sight,
Crying for help where the snow's grained white
Sifts over into dark.
                              His parents come;
Men ladder out across the ice,
Shouting when they find the hole, but he is gone
Far down below the reasoned town
Where suddenly the shops close twice
Because he's drifting underneath
A surface where his father's breath
Clouds everything but death.
That's how it happens, muted, brief,
And fittingly cold; we tell it over
To ourselves and to each other
Because it pulls us back again
This side of what no man
Has ever laddered over with a name . . .
A riddle, a story, a children's game.

The Covined Bird

. . .

The story told was how, before
He settled, my father hunted land
He'd never seen and wound up lost.
Walking a creek through uncut woods,
He found a lean-to built against
A bank, door opened, furniture inside,
Nothing else. It was cold, raining,
And getting dark, so he slept there—
Not on the rope bed or in a chair
But on the floor beside a trunk.

Next day, he shot a turkey hen,
"Dishragged her," he said. The bird had flown
Straight down on him; he raised, first shot,
The pellets gutted her midair.
He hung his kill, bleeding its throat,
Then built a fire and plucked it clean,
Saving the smoothest feathers from
What he later called his covined bird.
When I was small and sick for a long time,
He used to spread those feathers on my bed.

He hadn't eaten since he left his camp
The day before. The bird he killed
Was all the game he'd seen, and it
Had flown into his sights as if
Somehow angling home for him.
He'd heard its chalked-wood muttering
Before it flew, had searched for others
It must have called, but there was nothing.
Reluctant in an unknown house,
He cooked outside, but rested near the door,

Then slept a while, feeling himself
Rise and sink like someone breathing water.
Waking, he heard his bird's chalked cries again,
Coming from in the house. He waited;
One ear set to the stilled interior,
The other to the creek etching from sight,
There was no mistake in what he heard.
He stood, walked in, heard nothing there—
Stepped out, the calling started up.
He eased back in, looked carefully;

Found nothing again. The place he skipped
Was the trunk, too clearly someone else's,
But that was where he found the thing.
Inside, a boy at least three feet,
Dried to perfection; he'd seen this once
In school and thought nothing of it,
But here was a child age four or so
With wrapping twine sewn in his belly,
Where someone had either stabbed him
Or tried to save him, likely both.

Already middle-aged, a doctor,
He'd seen enough to weather this,
But didn't; settling to the floor,
He stared, then felt himself recede
From that house, the woods, everything.
Then he was back, got up, found a soft
Indentation in the bank and deepened it,
Wrapped the small mummy in his shirt
And buried it under a pile of stones,
A private cairn, but to no reckoning.

Working south from the house and creek,
He climbed up to a logging trail
Then turned due west, following ruts
Now barely visible, but the path
Played out into another uncut wood
So he started back the other way.
Passing where he found the trail, he saw
A trace of smoke angling from the lean-to,
Another hunter, or something else.
He didn't stop to see what followed there

But walked on out to where his trail
Turned to a dirt road that ran downhill
And fed into a blacktop road.
He hitched a ride to the main camp,
Packed his gear, said nothing to his friends,
And drove back home. That was fifty years ago.
He hunted several places then—
Fiery Gizzard, Cold Creek, Dead Tree . . .
Places I've never seen but where
I know you're better lost than caught.

He said that we were given back to him
For what he killed along that creek
And in the house; it was a rush of air
That's only heard inside a hollow place,
Something he knew but hadn't met,
As if he'd slept inside that house before
Moving familiarly, touching his way
Between two kinds of sleep, the one
Deep and generous, the other waiting
Like a fear born long before its name.

Water

. . .

How can we own a thing that travels
Constantly, evaporates, clouds over,
Rains back and pools,

                or else sinks,
Each fold or fault distorting its movement
In ways no sense of gravity predicts?
And how can we know the lateral habits
Of water, an immigrant who cannot
Settle anywhere, but circles over
Landscapes, erodes every border,
Edges shorelines of immeasurable sand.

Etched banks can channel it,
The current cutting deeper down,
Driving itself from underneath,
No longer water then but the force
Of gravity gathering its weight.
A watershed deflects the rain,
Or water table drops from use,
The downhill graduals of streams,
Spring floods and overflowing dams—
All tributaries feeding down
Into one long revisionary river
That curls against itself as if
The only way to move ahead
Was by deflecting back,
Like a language that explains itself,
A story told,

             this time about water.

The Hand-me-down

His father's clothes embarrass him
Like the five o'clock shadow that
Darkens his smile when he comes home
Carrying the bundled shirts and hat

Sent him as if to ask, "Where were you?"
They lump the whole event into
A wrinkled emptiness that shapes
Like rounded shoulders; someone waits

Ceremonious and still inside
Those folded sleeves, once opened wide.
Daphnis, Persephone, Adonis,
Atthis, Orpheus—all come to this:

The dying sex that promises return
Like spring, cut flowers, is a wreath that burns
As brightly as it disappears
Around its empty center.

Knowing there is no out, he calls
Things in, homing an animal
Scared of itself because it dies
Momently back into familiar eyes.

All mourning is inheritance,
Brief similarities and distance
In the very place he stands
Broken by what reaches his hand.

Driving Out

Some roads never pass beneath you
But waver like a focus held too long,
And you, the driver who can't turn his head,
Must look ahead and wait for trees to pass
And houses with their softened lights
To stream a quiet corridor.

Gears mesh. Your five good wheels turn round,
But the road outruns you. Accelerating,
You stall into the things you see . . .
As the road always narrows to
That one withdrawing point that is the point
You only reach by coming to a stop.

Meanwhile, your children walk, walk farther, leave,
And then return with children of their own;
While you were just about to clear your drive,
Turning into that same glassed road
That never widens underneath the hood
Or threads out of your mirror.

The engine idles evenly;
The radio still plays its songs;
And then someone announces war,
Great market shifts, a hurricane
That friends will chart at parties. You listen.
How disaster gives a voice authority!
You simply don't feel like going on.
You listen to another song.

The Name
. . .

With an easiness we almost learn . . .
Like the isolated shadow of a palm
Or variegated light by which a fern
Casts the lattice of its green calm—
Two workers lift in place a new fountain
For the courtyard in the starched hotel
Where, retired, my parents visited and remained.
Now, there's little here of them to tell,
Except that they were happy spending
Their days in shops, or walking the battery
When evenings cast outlines of the ending
They treated with such baroque finality.
Old clothes outgrew them, though their profiles changed
As imperceptibly as the courtyard
Where, year after year, they still arranged
Small gatherings and monitored
Their guests like two strict preservationists.

For years they did the ordinary thing—
The suburbs in a haze, high hedge and smoke
From cigarettes and grill, bluffed twinings
Overhead, rising beyond the jokes,
Choked laughter, and descending ice
Poured from lilting pitchers . . . premium gin
Precise as medicine.
                            And twice,
Promotion or the market up—some win—
The two of them waltzed across the patio
Laughing, we children laughing, not knowing why,
As the afternoon turned evening like a slow
Fade-out under a canvas sky.

There was a game we played in which
One child held a flashlight and one a mirror,
Attacker and attacked, the switch
Coming when, angled just right, the mirror
Blinded back, and then the game reversed. . . .
I think our parents played that way,
But differently, more slowly, and with words.
It was their means for setting things to stay,
Not out of differences or change
But somehow from the names they played
Back to one point—each view exchanged.

What brings me to this hotel now
Is a kind of stalled curiosity
Opening out the way a pattern goes
From holding its geometry
To something wider.
                              Crisp habits raise
Their own squared world, but lack
The final fact, when every gaze
Becomes the other view. The child
Looks up and back, then looks ahead
Beyond his own eroding ground, wild
As a nightmare's cranking landscape of the dead,
Where he calls the names he knows but no one wakes.
There water is the only constancy;
It fills headlong whatever way it takes,
Channeling a deep redundancy
As it steadies where its banks divide
Wider with floods, higher with drought.
For me that landscape was the side
Of a failing wall, a fountain's spout
Widening as I listened to regret
Coiling and uncoiling like a chain
Linking everything it touched. It let
Me stand once, balanced like a name,
Realizing how the water fell by rising,
How what it brought and took away were the same.

Dr. Williams' Garden

for Paul Mariani

A city, a mountain, a river,
And somewhere else a garden snake
Mildly frightening to the child
Who steps across its length before
It disappears into the grass. . . .

The snake recedes in memory
The way the child explains what he has seen,
Detail distancing detail until
The snake cannot return but must become
Another city, mountain, river;
And somewhere else the child has grown
Into a man who cannot say
What he has seen without his losing it.

And so he says it thing by thing,
Knowing that the words will leave him
Bankrupt beyond all tragedy,
As he stands beside a waterfall
Remembering the lusty heart
Of a fetus lost, or the sick heart
Of the young father who looked at him
And, buttoning his shirt, said nothing—.
A city, a mountain, a river
And everything still left to do
By a man whose feet go so unevenly
Over such uneven grass and accident,
That love must be a waterfall
Beside which good balance is belief.

The Starlings
. . .

Morgan's Steep, 1986

Not what they were but how they moved.
As if migration answered their cries,
Though no one call had meaning past
Its echo in another call.
They swept through trees like leaves blown back,
Like divinations ushered from before,
So many dividing against one breath . . .
The stillness, bluffed flights, the gliding down.

Above their sweeping fans, a hawk
Circled patiently, but they were thousands.
What he counted never counted him . . .
So many lifting, lighting.
                    And then they were gone.

But what they left they changed, the land
A silent dun without their cries,
Which, briefly, made the way the trees
Unfolded upward to the sky
Seem more than one place, more than one gathering
That in departing raised itself
As if some mute necessity
Had called its children not home but away.

. . .

II

To Be Sung on the Fourth of July

· · ·

We come to this country
By every roundabout,
With hunger like a startled face
And passports folding doubt,

With leaving home as commonplace
As children waking clear,
And hopeful as a fishline cast
Deep from the harbor's pier

To the idea of a country,
The garden and the name,
And a government by language
Called the New Jerusalem,

Where the trees have figured upward
As much as shadowed down;
And when we stood beneath them
We hugely looked around,

Because our gift is figures
That turn along our thought,
The apple, rock, and water,
The ram suddenly caught—

A country of inheritors
Who only learn of late,
Who set their eyes as blankly
As their livestock stand and wait,

There where the markets gabble
Till the bell has rung them home,
There where Chicago barters
The wheat crop for a loan,

Wait like the Cuyahoga
Floating tons of oil,
A city's burning river
And Cleveland set for spoil,

Wait like the black lake barges
That punctuate a course
Or linger in ellipsis
Between the yawning shores . . .

And then that huge interior
That always seems the same,
Abandoned wells, neglected fields,
And immigrants who came

Mapping the land they traveled for,
Stayed, worked a while, then died,
Or moved to cities where
They also worked and died

As, settlers who burned and built
And surveyed every line,
We timbered, plowed, and harvested
To songs in three-four time.

Our figures are like fireworks,
And water turned to fire;
In Cleveland or Chicago
The people never tire

Of the ballads of an innocence
That would not be dissolved,
But burned the witch and stuck like tar . . .
To the first citizen ever saved.

And though at times in chorus,
The music almost right,
We sing away the darkness
That makes a window bright,

In fact we're born too lucky
To see a street's neglect,
For the years have pushed us next to
An unalike Elect—

Who say the lost are with us
The way our backs go bad
Or eyes require new glasses
To peer into what's sad,

Which occupies the TV set
And functions by contrast,
Because well-being needs a grief
To make the feeling last.

Locals and Others

. . .

Jack Benny tells another joke
As Dinah Shore waves, driving out
To see the USA. This is the poke,
Pokey, and double time, the roundabout
Into flat roads stretching the way
Cartographers will tell you they will stretch . . .
Or thirty years ago it plays that way,
Flickering in a room where floor is catch,
And windows also catch, framing, each from
Its side, the black and white image that smiles
At unseen rooms, half-mortgaged homes,
Recliners aimed under strict ties and thin lapels.
Sometimes the president will stop and smile,
Or answer questions; soon his opened car
Speeding across the screen will stall
Into one image, zoomed close and blurred
And never focusing. And then there's color,
Red, green—as another story starts,
"Once upon a time, on a foreign chart". . . .
And I remember how men talked—
All Dinks or Slopes or Zipper Heads,
And Wes, who always made an oath
Out of his girl's father, who every month
Lost a finger to Charlie, for taxes,
Till they rigged a bomb. Always relaxed,
Wes, who attacked you if you woke him up,
And, once, while standing watch, tried to jump.

Retired to Minnesota, he writes
Old friends to say he can't forget
Three tours and plans to travel back
To "run down" his girl; and I think
For him the sidewalks are gray and absolute
Through what's become an early neighborhood.
Even the briefest laughter feels like years
Echoing in a house with no furniture,
A house where someone reads about
A stream that never runs from sight
Till thinking lets it ripple out . . .
That thought a kind of death, though not complete
For waking later, there is the rain—
First sounding the way the stream will run
Then building, like prolonged applause,
As if one little life could trump its laws,
Or free itself from that cold ellipsis
Where the figured God might place himself in us,
Mirrored briefly, balancing on a bank,
Then slowly fail to see our waving back.

Memorial Day

. . .

From shade to shade our neighbor mows
His civic way through the flexed spring grass,
Thick in its resurgent category
Of green, and widening from the eye.

He passes back and forth as if
Heard from a swing or hammock where
Someone almost asleep is letting
His motion sway the sound of things

Through an easy grazing pendulum
By which his season clocks itself . . .
While the grass is cut and kept from bearing seed
And the man will purchase what he needs

Of green, admixture bagged and weighed
Of every neighbor and his neighborhood,
Till it germinates from his scything wrist,
Who sews brief shadows, and in shadow rests.

1957
· · ·

That place where word breaks off into a call
Across the street, and an arm waves
Over the crowd. . . . Hello, good-bye, it says
Ushering itself, becoming small,
But never any farther than when
You first feel something winnowing
Each time you breathe. You hear it then,
That old exchange, as distancing
As people in a park who circle all day;
Some pause or slow, but no one stays,

No one waits late to see things forced, changed.
A boy once lost the stray dog he'd found
In the park beside our school. His voice strained
With calling its name. The older boys clowned
And mimicked him, some younger ones laughed. That was
Too long ago to tell just how it went,
But he was thin and stiff and, once he had paused,
He grew silent—his dog's name spent
On the older boys, who bunched like scrub trees,
But towering to him, as they broke his view
Into that inside world where what we see
Encircles us, says no, and is untrue.

Good Buses

. . .

No longer son but father now,
I watch the local buses work
Against their schedules to a stop
Where for the first time no one gets back on.
Wheels break for this; the papers sell,
Then blow into a sudden afternoon
As the tinted glass aligns against
The sun. The view reflects itself.
But what I see stays seated, adjusts,
Then settles back as the diesel's slow
Gathering forward blues the air.
The advertisements gust but no one looks,
Because going is not being there.

The Bed

. . .

The first one lasted thirteen years
And helped them get two children;
It sagged and angled gravity
And rolled the two of them together,
Peacefully fallen in their sleep
Where curling the same way every night
They shared his snoring, her chilly feet.
Now at forty, they buy another
And figure one more after that.
Two more rounds of breaking in and down,
At first the favored sag and then
The deep canal of their linked sleep
Deepening farther every year they keep
To the same old wager, he from his side,
She from hers, the mattress not so wide
Now but serviceable, as they reckon
Under the current spread, three score and ten.

The Actuarial Wife

. . .

for Patty

About their chances for divorce,
She says, "Slim—
Because the one who leaves
Will have to take the children."

About their children,
She says,
"We should have waited until
They were older to have them."

But most about her husband's smoking.
He's fifty now, and, taking stock
Of all they have, she stands outside
The blue haze through which he angles down
Into his favorite easy chair
Like an accurate punt, perfect hang time,
To read the morning paper over coffee
And start another pack of Luckies, stubbed
Emphatically, like punctuation marks
Down through an urgent argument.
She clarifies their options for retirement:
"Darling, if one of us dies,
I'm going to live in Paris."

Playing by Ear

Plunking the keys until sent out
To plunk anything that didn't resonate,
So, playing the sticks against a fence
And tremoring garbage cans with rocks . . .
Later, reaching the Zenith's off-on-
volume-switch, which twisted full circle,
Tubes warming, till the music dopplered
Like a headlong freight that didn't pass
And I was ushered out again. . . .
And what I learned was how things sound,
And that they sound so differently.

We had a mockingbird who came back year
After year, possessive, inventive,
Self-distancing inside his tree,
Where he built medleys from other voices—
Not like that corny radio star,
The Whistler, whose melody and pitch
Dried on his lips with selling manuals
So you could whistle after.
                              For him,
You were a silence.
                    But for the small fierce bird
Others were a threat he warned away
By mimicry. You heard yourself,
And knew to be afraid.
                      And that is how
You play by ear, self-separating,
Like allegory from the other side,
Where the distance in a mimicked world
Is reason enough to make things hide.

The Fear

It is a rain that never stops
But threatens the depth of everything,
Gutters, sewers, sludged rivers thickening,
As it hazes your blue clarity
And angles in the eye, where you catch
Its unfamiliar mirroring of you,
Leaning, no chance to straighten back.
Also, it's accurate. Next door,
A dying woman's chain-stoke breathing
Echoes through a common ceiling vent;
From her adjustable bed she sounds
Metallic, breathing against herself,
Stopping, then catching up again until
Somewhere a 50s Buick, fluid drive,
Shifts automatically, then plays
Glissandos along her drive
                           and is gone
From where you sit late, too strange to be sorry,
Listening for the traffic out ahead,
Some siren or blaring horn to warn you back
Into a lane that's governed by
Luminous lines, edged lights, the U-turn sign
That lets you curl and start again.

The Circle Route

. . .

Return is what a thaw smells like,
A meadow's wide periphery and trace.
But no arrival settles in one place,
So brighten on your toes and look

Farther than you ever thought to go.
Air thins with going, as the émigré
Unfolds his map and reads but cannot say
How his leaving framed its own tableau.

What's light at first weighs with suspension,
Stretching what you walk; but hurried or slow,
You arrive in time, and peer into
Mute window-dress, your stalled reflection

Where you see that home was what you didn't know
And left as soon as learning;
For you were hurry and the door and go
And timeless in returning.

Home

. . .

It is a place you've never been
Or passing at a distance seen
And recognized as where you slept,
Nursed, then slept again but somehow left

Without good-byes or one address
To get you back. Doors open less
Than give to what's behind them;
Home is like this, a clearing stream

Reflecting you and all you see, pushed on
By what must follow it alone
Yet multiple as numbers
That separate and join. There is no wonder

At the hall's dark end, a key that's tight
Against your hand or a blinding light
To find you out, or show you in;
There's only *home,* that word where you begin

Searching again for where you've never been.
Like smiles with teeth, it's where the bone
Breaks out, the fracture that you cannot set,
A language that does not forget.

The Only Child
· · ·

I know nothing is ever the same—
While you insist on likenesses,
That window, this picture, the common name
In families. It's differences
That keep us sane. Your mild reciprocals,
Golf, tennis at the local club, drinks, pals,
And maybe a story taken home . . .
But when you tell it you are alone;
The kitchen and the family room
Are not for narratives. They are too soon
About their ends; they know their lines,
Geometrize, subdue, define.
Or, here's likeness for you . . . like this—
Some salesman rings your bell and lists
The favors he is doing you
And just to get him lost you do
Exactly what he wants, chip in,
Buy the marvel prizing your one good hinge,
And turning away, relieved, realize for once
How little you wanted what you've got, once.
But that's too easy. What I mean
Is not "no," or "told you so," but green
For as long as it lasts, or is seen—
Green above, below, and you between, thinking,
"Nothing *is* the same," and that thought, too, winking.

The Lean and the Fat

. . .

Look up, look down,
look all around,
yous pants is falling down.

> *—David Bartlett*

Inflated like a clown's balloon,
We spiraled to another crash
Slap on the floor like uncooked meat—
This time a chicken but no pot, stone soup
With something for the stone, alive
And someone ringing necks in clockwise starts.

Now, fact is the whole house resonates
With fans, compressors, straining pipes—
Clamorous as a Spike Jones band
That blares, half strange, half comprehensible,
The white-noise cry of voices heard
Over the rusted hinge that bleats
Outside, where I walk our neighborhood
Of mortgages and widows, rents come due,
Screened windows sieving light to dark
And curtains hanging, dutiful
As the decent, well-intended lives
That pay for everything I see.

I walk our street of stripped treelawns,
Mailboxes with their numbers blurred,
Empty now, and awkward as the noise
That drove me out and drives me back
Again to everything at once,
Where suddenly the carpets are
Too intricate to walk across
And nothing can adjust the furniture's
Broken retreat along the wall.
Outside, an airplane's green and red,
Green and red blinks past but cannot change
As a single jet labors from sight
Like a shy man behind a cliché.

And like a Carnival's bright grief,
Blinking past January, I wait
For the start and stop by which we count,
And escape the count, watching like children
Stalled and edging the light that rings
The cartoon bubble where nothing's said . . .
Where parents, children, grandparents,
Sisters, brothers, their families,
The ones who died, although we held them
Hard enough to know they shouldn't die—
Where all stand in one brief telescoping line
Like travelers stunned with waiting.

Sometimes I take the car and estimate
An older, tireder neighborhood
Where everything approximates
An earlier boom and bust, sagged down
To something quiet and familiar
As an aging pet that's even lost at home,
Or a dull driver who, looking ahead,
Thinks what he thinks will stop with *now,*
Which sadly scurries under the hood
Into the curled map's larger scale.

And home—which never names the bending hello
Said after tilted hats across
The opened park . . .
                              high spirits and stout hope
Can't knot your tie or point your wing tips home;
That is the comic's rule and roost,
One last resolve that teases you
As jet trails dwindle out of sight
In the descriptive sky, where you
Check your roof and clean your gutters,
Feeling the weather change, like you,
In an irony that will not bend
Or cry beyond its own stilled laughter
Where someone, like you, buckles, forever
Trying to catch his breath again,
Either to start or to stop laughing.

Laughed out and out of breath,
I passed the forty-mile marker on
An interstate that had no exits
And glanced in the rearview mirror,
Finding myself gazing like Janus
Between one year's mute end and another,
All travel turned a common story . . .
As Eve to Johnny Appleseed.

Young enough that life still held
A secret prize, riding without hands
And reading the sign that says,
"You can't be first, but you can be the next,"
I ended on a residential drive,
Low overhead and long-term rates,
Where the boxwoods solidly affirmed
The surveyed lines that placed me on
The checkerboard, doubled my jump,
Took a round life and squared its hat
And taught me how to pocket change.

There's nothing bruised in Paradise, perhaps,
Where the elevators stall between
Your coming in or going out,
Leaving you happy, expectant, unspent
And ready for the avenues
That finger from the city into
That fattening land never seen
And never lost because it withdraws.
But here, the neighborhoods collapse with grief.
Change changes what you love and thins
Its face to what you cannot recognize,
As the round world flattens into facts
And the raw meat spoils forever.

. . .

III

Crosswords

Devoted to the compost pile,
She carried back their coffee grounds,
Odd table scraps the dog refused,
Rinds, cores, eggshells, old newspapers,
Until he said his will required
An open-casket funeral
To guarantee she'd bury him.

And when he died the garden ran
To weeds, wealthy under her homely
Ministrations wearing out the plot
She turned by years against more years,
Feeding her well-fed encumbrances—
Children, grandchildren, even pets
Brought home to pee, scratch, and chew the furniture.

At night she watched the news alone,
Then worked the crosswords into sleep;
Once she dreamed he spoke, praising their years,
And she saw small children standing still,
Waiting for the two of them to move.
But when she reached, it all was gone
Into a weather washed from sight

By a blue haze and blank dispersal
Vaster than any amplitude
The heart sounds out of its bruised range;
Leaves winked the sun, and a shallow light
Washed under trees as if the tide
Of their green mass curled over her
Saying, "The only thing you loved was change."

Late Days

· · ·

Late light across a side porch where
Two people play canasta—laugh,
Shuffle, talk, then deal the decks and stare
As if the cards, played out, will graph
Their afternoon, their working out
A private rhetoric, some stance
Each pauses over like a bet
Without debate, a preference
That carries them forward yet narrows
As the house bulks white against its shadow.

And as they stall above their game
Their laughing tears among the trees,
Echoing distances with names
That drift alone among the leaves
As they loosen wildly but color down,
Graceful in the quilting avenues
That settle as the season drowns
Along the ground, until the shade subdues
Their laughter, loosening like a weight
That drops where now they touch and hesitate.

Recalling Summers
· · ·

Towhead, stubbed toe, the stubble ground
That combines leave, sharp to the hand
And dry as August heat . . . what comes back now
Pauses like a stubborn catfish saying no
To every question mark dropped upside down,
Where the best bait's struck before it drowns.

Long afternoons when nothing breathed,
The deep indented paraphrase of waiting
When no one came . . . and the stillness, an upraised
Ladder where I wavered, balancing,
Or fell because I was afraid
That what the ladder lifted came unmade.

There was no elevated ease called *home*,
No coming in for good, but going out,
Till only one was one was one—
When the changes came, sudden as a shout
And numbing to touch, cold commonplace . . .
Like all those photographs we smiled to face.

For Don, Who Slept through the War

When I was young, waking my uncle
Was dangerous; his fists flew everywhere,
Like a stunt man falling. No angle was safe.
I stood at a distance, or in the door,
And called with mock authority,
Until, arms pumping, he rose from his
Elected hibernation, groggy as
Spring's obligatory bear.
                         Now dead
For thirteen years. And I have turned
The age he was when I first woke him up,
Saying no to sleep and laughing
At his startled arms and doughy eyes.
And waking, I have socked three things
In so many days—the bedside table,
The wall, my headboard.
                       I grieved for him,
Killed in his tent, heavily asleep
When the mortar fire walked through his camp
From a war so casual nobody called
With even mock authority.

But all domains reverse themselves;
Just one click left on the mortar sight,
He would have lived . . .
                   until at home
I too am stunned with waking when
I cannot see who calls, as staggering
Approximation of myself,
Stiff joints and eyes unfocusing,
I gather, unbuckling forward,
Smiling fuzzily and answering yes,
Yes, for as long as I possibly can.

Doing the Numbers

· · ·

She is five, but they will not add.
All afternoon we do the cards,
Take breaks and talk, but things are made
So separately that joining them is hard
Beyond belief. Later, she sleeps,
And, checking her, I find she's kept
The cards . . . as if they worked by guess
When, dreaming, she turns from somewhere to somewhere else.

The numbers haven't joined this time,
Though soon enough they will—the clichéd rhyme
All new again, as she adds one to one.
But for now, like Sleeping Beauty, she is alone.
I would keep her that way, briefly,
Because the numbers add relentlessly,
As the body forms a break through which
We think we walk a wider reach
Than home . . . though a landscape only seen.
It is this opening between
Two ways of looking, this resting gate,
That marks her now, where she hesitates,
Too young, still, to turn and wake—
Or, should she miscount, ever to escape.

With Others
. . .

Once capable of swimming the mile
In the low twenties, half adolescent
Into his years, he drove across
The pool as if the afternoon
Were permanent, some personal fixture
Stationed over his head, until
The sun clocked out of sight
And reckoned visible again
The way his house, chaise longue, and hedge
Shadowed wide of their tight plantings,
Brief geometric slights that played
Under an August constancy—graduals
Lengthening from their first places
On a bank that thickened and blanked the view.

It was the way he tired that told him
How far he'd gone, or had to go.
His graying head could tuck into
A stride or rounding dive and never look up;
Swimming, he planed and barely broke
The water's surface, head buried in
A blue he couldn't explain, merely
Traveled through, efficiently silent.
To us, his strength was a wealth he spent;
His spending was continuous.

What he gave up he gave away,
Glad impulse like a tightened wave
That curls high up but never crashes,
Only settles and recedes
Back to the body where it grew.
Lifted out of water into air,
He rose from one thing to another
Until he called good-bye to us
From his wide hospital window.
We watched him waving quietly,
A gesture meant beyond itself
In a window opened east without a shade.

Men lose their wills to something more than will,
A widening across fixed distances
They thought to hold accountable,
Their lives one long immeasurable gesture
That gives back all it ever grasps
In the extended summer light
Of an afternoon with others.

The Blue Umbrella

• • •

This is not about the barrenness of winter,
A single bird fluting that tired song,
But another melody, caught just before
Our voices turn to words, or faces flex
Expression, then drift the way a viewer's eyes
Fatigue just as the reel plays out, the film
Raking its last black edge over and over
Against a screen that's now a concrete wall.

It is about a landscape we project
Backward, recalling our habit of walking
Separately yet talking as we scuff
The brush before the wind hurries it past
Our idiom—land, sky, each other,
A repeated phrase that makes the season
Familiar, like a favorite story
Told to children afraid and needing sleep.

Blue before blue, we predicate our sky
Over a landscape lost in measurements
Until in loss we take the thimble way,
The light seed spiraling down, back to
That place the children's story starts,
Where color is a parasol
Because the sun's too bright to see.
Light gathers in the blue umbrella;

The sun balances from an upheld arm.
Wrinkling dark, like circles under eyes,
It shadows our standing here together,
Where when we called our stories make-believe
We turned that thought against itself,
So many of us lost, so many new,
And recognized each other then
Speaking out of a plenitude
In which no one imagined more.

Good-bye

. . .

for John and Laura

Whatever we are, we're torn like strips
Of cloth, and knotted together against
A wind whose changes are our directions
Read backwards, tugging away from where,
Facing, we watch ourselves fluttering home
From what the eye's transparency engulfs—
All we ever thought, because what we thought
Is there, *is* given, yet leads us back,
Though not to one place but to one starting out.
This is good-bye; this breaks the heart.

Because we are a knot that stops itself,
A thing that holds the way a seed
Carried by air beyond its origin
Catches and swells till its economy
Enfolds another starting out,
We are a script within a later script,
Written for light, air, earth, and water
In a place made out of openness.
We make it our common place,
Our origin all over again.

Look deeper through that place and watch
The leaf unfolding as the root unfolds,
Till later, the green, outreaching limbs
Fan beneath a sky rounding from sight
As if each branch's shades were something whole,
Growing to every part. No line divides;
Leaf, limb, and seed—the trunk that holds
Such branching thought up green against
Our circumfused first questioning,
This is our first analogy.

Below the trunk, the root takes hold,
Thickens, and burrows out of sight,
A blank albino thirsting downward,
Like our Fall again, self-separating
And hungry as our nakedness.
Whatever leaf we took to cover that
Turned into sickness and to death—
A mother's pain, and food by sweat
Out of a grudging field whose furrows
Approximate the way we end.

Good-bye waved out our generation
Through a jungle's underbrush; limbs broke
With boys stiffened against the thing
They saw when shaving, themselves reversed,
Like fathers, framed in a bristled force
That felt like want. They never wanted what
Those fathers meant, night watches where
The enemy was every breathing leaf,
A rhetoric of sudden silences,
And opposites who aimed good-bye.

My daughter bleeds because good-bye
Has turned her so, her temperament
Rebelling against a self-betraying
Innocence in which she is caught,
Asking, who asked for this? Her mother splits
With telling why, so many ways—
The cramp that swells and also splits
Into another openness,
Crying with hunger. Cries muffled
Like a covered seed the heart enfolds.

It is the comic's clipped delivery,
Good-bye . . . his joke shut down
On someone tagged before first base.
Deadpan and perfect timing, he leads
Us through the incongruities
Of fat, stingy, dumb. The fat laugh loudest.
The lights turned down to anonymity,
We follow what is done to others—
Laughing, "We are not you; we are not like you
But are ourselves," until the laughter dies.

Good-bye is a child's clean slate on which
Someone must write his name repeatedly,
Or else he cannot free himself
From a room in which the walls breathe
Like a resting animal, or whale
That vomits up a god's scared messenger,
Caught between the words he's made to say
And his terror over saying them,
His language like a desert wind, audible
Against the tree, tower, or town that resists.

And it is like our other self
Hung threadbare on a tree to suffocate.
Our language breathes him back again;
But no matter how we try, the story
Recoils into its first recorded facts,
Our telling it sometimes as predatory
As any time we ever killed
And made it true. We eat and drink
Good-bye collectively, and call
It love by a raveling tale.

Good-bye is the beginning that
We never knew, the fruit at once ripe
And green, torn mother with her kneading child.
It is a landscape we are homesick for
But have never seen, a place projected
Out of need. We tear plain cloth,
Tie knots, and watch the wind ribbon us back.
Myth, song, a fruitful place to pause . . .
We arrive out of our terrible freedom
Which kills and loves us like a starving mother.

The Lake House
. . .

They water-ski over whitecaps
The wind tops up on a man-made lake
Outside Atlanta.
                    The water widens
Green to blue where their slaloms sculpt
Brief arcs around peninsulas
Jutting out of red-banked Georgia.
It's 1969. She salutes
Left-handed, shading her eyes,
Watching successive skiers pass
And diminish where their wakes fan out;
Then the sun brightens, fixed things waver,
So she turns from her pier and walks into
The cool of a stone summer house.
The skiers crisscross back and forth,
Arms straightened to the ski rope's tug,
Tanned bodies angling back through curve
After curve, rhythmical, as if
Some gradual was silently towing them
Across a plain balanced between
Two bells,
                the earth cupped upward,
The sky cupped down,
                      and water deepening
Blue into blue beyond focus.

Inside, the house stills everything,
Its rooms a series of silences
Arranging furniture, each with
Its view, the lake, a picture window
Squaring another set of silences—
Skiers rounding beyond the window's frame,
Elliptic where they cut high rooster tails
Repeated like a child's toy that's wound,
Released, then wound again.
In the last room down the hall a boy's things
Stand boxed, dated years ago.
                                    He's flying now
Over Southeast Asia; what's left behind
Are flags, biplanes, a train, bright cars,
And on the ceiling
                        stars arranged
In tiny constellations, Serpens,
Perseus, Andromeda, Orion . . .
Placed in a circle so, "Lights Out,"
He could lie on his back and navigate
Across a ceiling as close and clear
As the luminous face of his father's watch,
His father gone, flying for Nimitz
And Bull Halsey.
                        That ceiling never altered;
Its bright particulars were fixed points of
A boy's departure, small geometries
Set wide against his fear of sleep.

At school he heard the Japanese
Stretched prisoners on bamboo shoots
Then walked away, indelicate
To hear the screams, as the green shafts
Drove up in dark, reaching for light
Till the ground was still and green again.
And then Hiroshima, Nagasaki.
But nothing changed. No one returned.
Beside the cracked, concrete highway to town,
Stone Mountain's half-completed generals
Rode south with Lee, as if the next few steps
Might break them free of their locked origin.
Weekends, the Piedmont Driving Club . . .
Golf, tennis, the pool, or Fox Theater,
And Peachtree Street's dogwoods in bloom—
Then Ponce de Leon Avenue
Unraveling late light through pines,
Curving into 1969
When he's not thought of bamboo shoots
For years, or needed stars fixed overhead
To get to sleep, his missing father
Stalled in shallow spirals,
Wings angling a glide path home
But his Corsair never "touching down."

This is a story about a story,
Two times at once because a woman
Opens her lake house for the summer;
Moving from room to room, she cleans
Windows, gauging her strict horizon
As it distends outside on water,
A litany of successive nows
In which her son and husband stand,
Both young, and thus their lives
Going separately at once, as they
Angle away, two large, high-noon shadows
That never meet.
     She almost prays,
Saying, "If only for a moment,
Let my thinking take the place
Of their two absences so that
I see them here again, the water
Buoying their energetic waves
As, banking, they ski beyond this lake
Into one bright, continuous curve
Back home, where they dwell again in me."

Their dwelling hollows every room.
Turning, she thinks the sunlight's best
For plants in corners, there urging her ferns
And dieffenbachia up to the clean,
Cool edges of her windowsills
That let onto the water's glaze.
Outside, the lake steadies the day.
Inside, her gaze extends to where
The sky and water meet, a draftsman's line,
The water rising into its opposite.

One opposite confers another.
Sometimes she starts half-stunned because
The skiers lean through curves the way
Her son has learned to shoulder his plane.
She wonders if someway he thinks
He'll find his father out ahead
Caught in one last acrobatic roll
Beneath a Zero tailing him
Like a tireless predatory bird
He cannot see because the sun's
Behind the plane, only a glint
Above before it fires on him
Still in his roll, arching upward
But looking down, two waiting cups,
Two blues identical and wide
Of thought.
                    There's nothing up or down,
As their son, one wing away, alert,
Tightens into his own high-speed shedding
That is terror banking into itself.
She is dusting but, seeing this,
Hunches till her hands let go,
Then stares because she's dropped a glass
Between her feet, its tiny fragments
Scattered in a soft blue constellation
Patterning the place she stands, uncertain
What she was doing, or what she will do.
Beyond the house, only the light shatters
Where the wind cuts up the lake like glass
Reflecting upward in a thousand pieces.

Rio

. . .

This down by which we go runs like
One thought. Great river barges widen it
Into a traffic silent and slow
As any growth that took a body
To its maturity or quiet end.
With evening, cool running lights
Practice direction but never change,
Two ways to go but only one leads out.
For some, the river's merciless and pure
As an upland thawing stream
Where gravity is headlong and heedless,
Until there's nothing bent, only what bends;
For others, it is a mother slow and sorrowful
Murmuring her missing children's names,
Names lost like objects dropped, sedimented,
Or like trapped gestures, articulate and bright
On a silted bed that never settles.

Each tide an estuary toward the moon,
The moon a rounding back into its tide,
The lost idea imagines us all new again . . .
Until its tributaries widen to
One current where a river cuts
Its way, less narrow as it goes,
And the last of it never closing off
But something like the mother fish
Whose mouth collects her young, then lets them out again,
As if she spoke her children into life.

Some stories have no end but tell us out
Into an opening where, turning, we
Begin repeatedly, listening
As our telling takes away and gives
Us all we ever had, missed, believed.
Having and not having is how we go,
Like hope beyond reason . . . some lost thing found
Become a gift because we had forgotten
Where it was, a gift out of
Two ownerships, a rich recovery.

Too long at sea, too little time on shore,
Glass raised and nothing left to raise
Except the silent ways the people found
To join and separate . . . handshake, half-wave
From the Bondé on the viaduct . . .
What I recall was comical and cruel,
The dirt and wealth of Rio during Carnival—
Blown papers kiting up, the smog,
Crisp sails of ocean-going racers
Singling in from the Cape Town Race.

Along the streets impromptu bands
Arranged themselves, blared, settled, marched,
Gradually building a following;
The traffic stopped, police and drivers
Studying the masks that nodded past them
Down one long contrapuntal avenue
Wide as a city block and full
Of bright, gaudy, exaggerated faces.

High laughter is a cry sustained,
And painted masks are many cries at once
When women dance their own round mobile,
Balancing their grinning lamentations.
But on a terrace above the bay,
Two people slipped into a samba,
And nothing steadied where they stepped;
The music was anatomy
Bodied forth in easy choruses
Like a tropical ease that shouldered them,
Until they moved so strictly opposite
They rounded everything, yet gazed
Into some middle ground that dulled their eyes.
They danced before the rest, earlier
And balancing against the bay
As the half-cocked moon bled everything . . .
The water, sand, Avenida Atlántica,
Even the dirt-pathed *favelas*
That bunched in quiet distances,
Almost toppling, as pricked from hillsides
With packing crates, odd boards, old signs,
They held the world to one story—
Up close, few lights, mostly the moon bland on
Corrugated roofs, by day too hot to touch
But now cool and subdued as those who slept
Or sat in doors to get a breeze
Round corners where small children played
Near naked bulbs that pocketed the dark.
The smallest of them wore no clothes,
And at the farthest reaches of the light
Their thin brown arms became invisible,
Fey as the grass fires that drove them to the coast,
Or as the tiny water organisms
That waited for their lives like thirst.

I watched the two who danced against the bay,
And knew that their distracted steps
Took them past the limits of the little towns
From which so many came, took everything
Beyond the scale of just endurance,
To where deserted animals will turn,
Circling out of the way, or people
Living on the street will sleep coiled up
As if they meant to wake running.
While beauty was the brief indifference
Of a dance, which I could only watch,
Thinking how strange it was to name
A river for a time, for explorers,
Not knowing where they were but when,
To say, Rio de Janeiro,
Naming departure for return—
Balancing a city that, bulldozing down
And scaffolding up the same cramped needs,
Was as angular and thin along the coast
As any new-world history . . .
While Guanabara Bay curved back
Into an arc of crowded avenues
That channeled inland like so many fingers
Pushed through a Carnival in which
Each dressed as someone else and all
Found their way a making way dividing where
They danced, as crowded and anonymous
As the *movimento* of their millions . . .
Each empty hand a plucking down;
But one by one so many lifting up.

Wyatt Prunty's other books of poetry, *The Times Between* and *What Women Know, What Men Believe*, are also available from Johns Hopkins. He is the author of a critical study of contemporary poetry, *"Fallen from the Symboled World": Precedents for the New Formalism*. His poems and essays have appeared in the *New Yorker, New Republic, Parnassus, American Scholar, Kenyon Review, New Criterion, Yale Review, Southern Review,* and *Sewanee Review*. He has taught at Louisiana State University, Washington and Lee University, Virginia Tech, Johns Hopkins University, and the University of the South (Sewanee), where he is the Carlton Professor of English.

Library of Congress Cataloging-in-Publication Data

Prunty. Wyatt.
  Balance as belief / Wyatt Prunty.
       p.   cm.—(Johns Hopkins, poetry and fiction)
  ISBN 0-8018-3893-2 (alk. paper). — ISBN 0-8018-3894-0 (pbk. : alk. paper)
  I. Title.   II. Series.
PS3566.R84B35   1989   89-33038
811'.54—dc20   CIP